DOG

Douglas Bender

TABLE OF CONTENTS

A Pelican Book

Teaching Tips for Caregivers and Teachers:

Research shows that one of the best ways for students to learn a new topic is to read about it.

Before Reading

- Read the title and predict what the book will be about.
- Read the "Words to Know" and discuss the meaning of each word.
- Read the back cover to see what the book is about.

During Reading

- When a student gets to a word that is unknown, ask them to look at the rest of the sentence to find clues to help with the meaning of the unknown word.
- Motivate students with praise and encouragement.

After Reading

- Discuss the main idea of the book.
- Ask students to give one detail that they learned in the book.

SIGHT WORDS

a
all
and
are
big
can
do
eat
have
is
like
little
some
this

WORDS TO KNOW

dog

dog food

tails

treats

tricks

This is a **dog**.

dog

Some dogs are big,
and some are little.

All dogs eat **dog food**.

dog food

Some dogs can do **tricks**!

trick

Some dogs have **tails**.

tails

All dogs like **treats**.

treats

INDEX

Written by: Douglas Bender
Design by: Under the Oaks Media
Series Development: James Earley
Editor: Kim Thompson

Photos:
Shutterstock: ESB Professional: cover; xkundova: p. 5; Alberto Hernandez Leva: p. 7; Alex_ugalek: p. 9; dezy: p. 11; ayorch: p. 13; Javier Brosch

Library of Congress PCN Data
Dog / Douglas Bender
My First Pet
ISBN 978-1-63897-429-1(hard cover)
ISBN 978-1-63897-544-1(paperback)
ISBN 978-1-63897-659-2(EPUB)
ISBN 978-1-63897-774-2(eBook)
Library of Congress Control Number: 2022932419

Printed in the United States of America.

Seahorse Publishing Company
www.seahorsepub.com

Published in the United States
Seahorse Publishing
PO Box 771325
Coral Springs, FL 33077